MY
Grandma's
Life Story

Keepsake
Journal

THIS BOOK
BELONGS TO:

....

....

About This Journal

THIS JOURNAL IS ABOUT YOUR JOURNEY—ONE FILLED WITH LOVE, LAUGHTER, AND MOMENTS THAT HAVE SHAPED WHO YOU ARE. IT'S A WAY TO HONOR THE AMAZING MOM YOU ARE.

THE BOND WE'LL ALWAYS SHARE

NO MATTER HOW MUCH TIME PASSES, OUR BOND REMAINS UNBREAKABLE. EVERY PAGE OF THIS JOURNAL IS A REMINDER OF THE LOVE AND MEMORIES WE SHARE.

YOUR QUIET STRENGTH

YOU'VE ALWAYS BEEN OUR ROCK, EVEN WHEN THINGS GOT TOUGH. THIS JOURNAL LETS YOU REFLECT ON THOSE EVERYDAY ACTS OF LOVE AND STRENGTH—THE ONES THAT MAY SEEM SMALL BUT MEAN THE WORLD TO US.

FROM US, WITH LOVE

FILL THESE PAGES WITH YOUR THOUGHTS, MEMORIES, AND WISDOM. IT'S OUR WAY OF SAYING THANK YOU FOR EVERYTHING, AND A REMINDER THAT YOUR STORY AS A MOM IS TRULY SPECIAL.

YOUR JOURNEY IS ONE-OF-A-KIND, AND WE HOPE THIS JOURNAL HELPS YOU CELEBRATE EVERY BEAUTIFUL PART OF IT.

Dear Grandma,

Though I've known you all my life, I want to truly understand the full story of who you are. I'd love for you to share your life's journey with me.

As we go through these pages, my hope is that you'll reflect on your memories and be as open and honest as you can, so I can hold onto the moments and stories that have shaped you.

This journal will forever hold a special place in my heart, capturing everything that makes you uniquely you.

TELL ME YOUR STORY

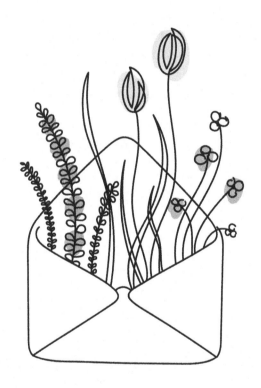

Love you Grandma!

MILESTONES

ABOUT YOURSELF

DETAILS ABOUT YOU

FULL NAME	DATE OF BIRTH

PLACE OF RESIDENCE	HEIGHT

EYE COLOR	HAIR COLOR

ABOUT YOURSELF

"The story of your birth is the beginning of your life's greatest adventure."

Is there a special meaning or story behind why your parents chose your name?

_____

_____

_____

_____

_____

What was your length and weight at birth?

_____

In what city were you born?

_____

_____

Were you born in a hospital or somewhere else?

_____

_____

_____

ABOUT YOURSELF

"The day you were born, the world received a beautiful gift."

Were you a healthy baby, or were there any health concerns?

_____

_____

_____

How old were your parents when you were born?

_____

How old were you when you took your first steps?

_____

What were your first words?

_____

What did your parents say you were like as a baby?

_____

_____

_____

_____

Tell Me Your Favorites:

1   What is your favorite scent/smell?

2   What is your favorite place in the whole world?

3   What is your favorite color?

4   What is your favorite flower?

5   What is your favorite food?

Tell Me Your Favorites:

6   What is your favorite dessert?

7   What's your favorite brand of clothing?

8   What's your favorite season?

9   What's your favorite indoor / outdoor activity?

10   Who is your favorite singer?

Tell Me Your Favorites:

11   What is your favorite beverage?

12   What is your favorite way to relax after a long day?

13   What's your favorite holiday?

14   What's your favorite thing to do with your family?

Grandma

[grandmother, friend] noun

The person who loves you unconditionally and fills your life with warmth and wisdom. The one who always has time to listen, share a story, and offer a gentle smile.

The woman who inspires me with her strength and kindness. My biggest cheerleader. My Grandma, who I am blessed to call my dear friend.

2

YOUR
CHILDHOOD
YEARS

YOUR CHILDHOOD YEARS

"The stories of our childhood shape the people we become, cherished memories that stay with us forever."

How would you describe yourself as a little kid?

_____

_____

_____

_____

_____

_____

_____

_____

Did you have a nickname when you were
growing up? If so, how did you get it?

_____

_____

_____

_____

_____

_____

YOUR CHILDHOOD YEARS

"In the places we grow up, we leave footprints of innocence, laughter, and dreams."

Where did you grow up?

_____

Tell me about how you learnt to swim.

_____

_____

_____

_____

When did you learn to ride a bike? Who taught you?

_____

_____

_____

What kind of chores or responsibilities did you have at home?

_____

_____

_____

_____

YOUR CHILDHOOD YEARS

"The simple joys of childhood are the treasures we carry with us, no matter how much we grow."

What was your favorite book or story as a child?

_____

_____

_____

_____

_____

What was your favorite toy or game as a child?

_____

_____

_____

_____

What were the TV shows you looked forward to every week? Why you liked it?

_____

_____

_____

_____

YOUR CHILDHOOD YEARS

"The journey of learning is marked by favorite subjects, inspiring teachers, and unforgettable moments."

What was your favorite subject in school? Why?

_____

_____

_____

_____

What was your least favorite subject in school? Why?

_____

_____

_____

_____

Did you ever get into big trouble at school? What happened?

_____

_____

_____

_____

_____

_____

_____

YOUR CHILDHOOD YEARS

"In childhood, our fears are as big as our dreams, and our talents bloom with boundless imagination."

Did you have a favorite teacher? What made them special or memorable?

_____

_____

_____

_____

_____

_____

Were you into sports or music? If so, what did you play, and what was it like?

_____

_____

_____

_____

_____

_____

YOUR CHILDHOOD YEARS

"The warmth of family gatherings and shared traditions nourishes our hearts and memories."

Can you describe what a typical family dinner
was like? What did you usually talk about?

_____

_____

_____

_____

_____

_____

Did you have any family traditions or celebrations
that were important to you?

_____

_____

_____

_____

_____

_____

YOUR CHILDHOOD YEARS

"Looking back, the simple things hold the most meaning,
especially when shared with family."

Did you get an allowance when you were growing up? How much was it, and what did you like to spend it on?

_____

_____

_____

_____

Looking back, do you still remember how much these items used to cost?

- A gallon of milk: _____
- A loaf of bread : _____
- A movie ticket : _____
- A cup of coffee : _____
- A box of cereal : _____
- A newspaper : _____
- A hamburger : _____
- A haircut : _____
- A pair of jeans : _____
- One Year College Tuition: _____

YOUR CHILDHOOD YEARS

"The laughter of friends and the joy of celebrations create
memories that stay with us forever."

Who were some of your closest friends growing
up? Do you still talk to any of them?

_____

_____

_____

What did you and your friends do for fun after
school or on weekends?

_____

_____

_____

How did you celebrate your birthdays as a kid?
Do you remember a particularly special birthday?

_____

_____

_____

_____

YOUR CHILDHOOD YEARS

"Every childhood holds a little mischief, a few adventures, and memories to last a lifetime."

Do you have any fond memories of a family trip?

_____

_____

_____

_____

_____

_____

_____

_____

_____

_____

_____

_____

_____

YOUR CHILDHOOD YEARS

"Childhood is the most beautiful of all life's seasons, filled with laughter, mischief, and unforgettable moments."

Did you have any pets growing up? Tell me about them.

_____

_____

_____

_____

_____

_____

Do you remember the biggest time you got in trouble with your parents for something mischievous?

_____

_____

_____

_____

_____

_____

YOUR CHILDHOOD YEARS

"In the small, joyful moments of childhood, we find memories that warm our hearts forever."

Can you share a funny or heartwarming story from your childhood that still makes you smile?

_____

_____

_____

_____

_____

_____

_____

_____

_____

_____

_____

_____

_____

YOUR CHILDHOOD YEARS

"The scents, sounds, and simple joys of childhood linger with us, painting vivid memories in our hearts."

What smells remind you of your childhood?

_____

_____

_____

_____

If you could be born again, would you want to be a girl again or a boy? Why?

_____

_____

_____

_____

_____

_____

_____

_____

YOUR CHILDHOOD YEARS

Growing up is mandatory, but growing old is optional." – Walt Disney

What was your biggest fear as a child?

_____

_____

_____

_____

_____

What is one thing you really miss about being a kid?

_____

_____

_____

_____

_____

_____

_____

_____

NOTES

"If nothing is going well, call your grandmother."

— ITALIAN PROVERB

YOUR
TEENAGE
YEARS

Your
Teenage Years

"Our teenage years are a time of self-discovery, where we start shaping the person we're becoming."

How would you describe yourself when you were a teenager?

_____

_____

_____

_____

_____

_____

What kind of student were you?

_____

_____

_____

_____

_____

_____

Your Teenage Years

"Teenage years are a blend of daring fashion and finding where we belong, one style at a time."

What was your style like when you were a teenager? What were your favorite outfits and hairstyles?

_____

_____

_____

_____

_____

_____

_____

_____

What was the craziest fashion trend you followed as a teenager?

_____

_____

_____

_____

_____

_____

_____

_____

_____

Your
Teenage Years

*"In our teenage years, we push boundaries and experience
the thrill of newfound independence."*

Who were your best friends during your teenage years?
Are you still close with any of them?

_____

_____

_____

_____

What fun things did you do together?

_____

_____

_____

_____

_____

_____

_____

_____

_____

_____

Your
Teenage Years

"First crushes and bold moments make our teenage years memorable, filled with stories we hold close."

Did you have a curfew? What time was it, and what happened if you broke it?

_____

_____

_____

_____

_____

Did you ever sneak out of the house? Where did you go, and what did you get up to?

_____

_____

_____

_____

_____

_____

Your
Teenage Years

*"The things we never told our mothers often reveal how much
we didn't know about love and life."*

Who was your teen crush, or do you remember a
special date from that time?

_____

_____

_____

_____

_____

_____

_____

What was the most daring thing you did as a teenager that
your parents never found out about?

_____

_____

_____

_____

_____

_____

Your Teenage Years

"The hobbies and laughter of our youth remind us of the carefree joy we once knew."

What were some of your favorite activities or hobbies when you were a teenager?

_____

_____

_____

_____

_____

_____

What's a funny or embarrassing story from your teenage years that still makes you laugh?

_____

_____

_____

_____

_____

_____

_____

Your Teenage Years

"The responsibilities and mentors of our teenage years help guide us as we take on the world."

What clubs, sports, or activities did you participate in during school?

_____

_____

_____

_____

Did you have any mentors or role models as a teen? How did they impact you?

_____

_____

_____

_____

When did you get your first car? What was it, and who taught you to drive?

_____

_____

_____

_____

Your
Teenage Years

"The songs, movies, and events of our teenage years are like time capsules, filled with cherished memories."

What songs from high school bring back your favorite memories? Why?

_____

_____

_____

_____

_____

_____

What movie or TV show did you love as a teen? What made it special?

_____

_____

_____

_____

_____

_____

Your
Teenage Years

"Our teenage years are a mix of highs and lows, with each moment leaving an impression on who we become."

What were the best parts of your teenage years?

_____

_____

_____

_____

_____

_____

_____

What were the worst parts of your teenage years?

_____

_____

_____

_____

_____

_____

_____

_____

Your
Teenage Years

"The memories we're proudest of from our youth are the ones that shape our character and journey."

What's one thing you'd change about your teenage years if you could?

_____

_____

_____

_____

_____

_____

If you could give your teenage self one piece of advice, what would it be?

_____

_____

_____

_____

_____

_____

NOTES

NOTES

4

ABOUT YOUR PARENTS

ABOUT YOUR PARENTS

"The most beautiful thing about a mother's love is that even when she's gone, her love still guides us."

What is your mother's full name, and where did she grow up?

_____

_____

What three words would you use to describe her?

_____

_____

_____

What is one of your favorite memories with your mom?

_____

_____

_____

_____

_____

_____

_____

_____

ABOUT YOUR PARENTS

"A father's love may be quiet, but it speaks loudly through his actions and the legacy he leaves behind."

What is your father's full name, and where did he grow up?

_____

_____

What three words would you use to describe him?

_____

_____

_____

What is one of your favorite memories with your dad?

_____

_____

_____

_____

_____

_____

_____

_____

ABOUT YOUR PARENTS

"The story of how your parents met is the foundation of your family's love story."

In what ways do you think you're like your mom and
dad, and how are you different from them?

_____

_____

_____

_____

_____

_____

_____

Do you know how your parents met? Can you share the
story with me, as much as you remember?

_____

_____

_____

_____

_____

_____

ABOUT YOUR PARENTS

"A family recipe is a story of love, passed down from one generation to the next."

What family meal did your mom or dad make that you loved the most? Why does it hold a special place in your heart?

_____

_____

_____

_____

_____

_____

Can you share a simple version of the recipe?

_____

_____

_____

_____

_____

ABOUT YOUR PARENTS

"We carry pieces of our parents with us, and those pieces shape who we become."

Did your mom or dad have any special talents, like
singing, dancing, or fixing things?

_____

_____

_____

_____

_____

_____

_____

Do you have any unique cultural celebrations or
customs in your family?

_____

_____

_____

_____

_____

_____

_____

ABOUT YOUR PARENTS

*"The values and lessons we inherit from our parents shape the
foundation of who we become."*

How would you describe your family's financial situation
when you were growing up?

_____

_____

_____

_____

_____

_____

What was your relationship like with your parents
when you were growing up?

_____

_____

_____

_____

_____

_____

_____

ABOUT YOUR PARENTS

"The legacy of our parents is woven into the stories they leave behind and the lives they've touched."

What are some ways your parents showed they were proud of you?

_____

_____

_____

_____

_____

_____

What kind of legacy did your parents leave behind?

_____

_____

_____

_____

_____

_____

_____

ABOUT YOUR PARENTS

"The wisdom we carry from our parents is a gift that guides us, even when they're no longer by our side."

What's a memorable disagreement you had with your parents, and how did it turn out?

_____

_____

_____

_____

_____

_____

If you could spend one more day with a late family member, who would it be, and what would you do?

_____

_____

_____

_____

_____

_____

_____

ABOUT YOUR PARENTS

"In times of challenge, our family roots give us strength and resilience to carry on."

What's the best advice your mom or dad gave you, and
how did it shape your life?

_____

_____

_____

_____

_____

_____

_____

_____

_____

_____

_____

_____

_____

_____

_____

_____

NOTES

Grandmothers are the glue that holds everything together, with love as their secret ingredient.

ABOUT YOUR GRANDPARENTS

ABOUT YOUR GRANDPARENTS

"Even though you're no longer here, your love still guides us every day. We miss you more than words can say."

What's a memory with your grandparents that still makes you smile?

_____

_____

_____

_____

_____

What's the most special gift or keepsake you received from your grandparents?

_____

_____

_____

_____

_____

_____

ABOUT YOUR GRANDPARENTS

"Grandparents' recipes are written with love and passed down as treasured memories."

What's a special dish your grandparents made?

_____

_____

_____

_____

Was there something your grandparents did that always made you feel extra loved or special?

_____

_____

_____

_____

_____

Is there a favorite place you visited with your grandparents?

_____

_____

_____

ABOUT YOUR GRANDPARENTS

"In every cherished memory, we find a piece of you. Though you're gone, we carry your love in our hearts always. We miss you."

If you could spend one more full day with your grandparents, how would you like to spend it?

_____

_____

_____

_____

_____

_____

_____

_____

_____

_____

_____

_____

_____

_____

NOTES

SIBLING
[sib-ling] - noun

built-in partner in crime, who
you can always count on for a
good laugh and a shoulder to
cry on

ABOUT
YOUR
SIBLINGS

ABOUT YOUR SIBLINGS

"Through all the ups and downs, siblings are the ones who know us best."

How many siblings you have?

_____

List your siblings in order of age, including yourself, and
mention any funny nicknames they have!

_____

_____

_____

_____

_____

_____

_____

_____

_____

_____

_____

ABOUT YOUR SIBLINGS

"We didn't always see eye to eye, but we always stood heart to heart."

Which sibling did you fight with the most growing up, and why?

_____

_____

_____

_____

_____

_____

Which sibling were you closest to growing up, and why?

_____

_____

_____

_____

_____

_____

_____

ABOUT YOUR SIBLINGS

"You're my first friend and my forever friend."

What were your siblings like when they were kids?

_____

_____

_____

_____

_____

_____

_____

_____

How would you describe your bond with your siblings as a child?

_____

_____

_____

_____

_____

_____

ABOUT YOUR SIBLINGS

"No distance can break the bond we share."

Did you and your siblings have any special traditions or inside jokes?

_____

_____

_____

_____

_____

Do you remember a big fight with your siblings that your parents had to step in to resolve?

_____

_____

_____

_____

_____

_____

ABOUT YOUR SIBLINGS

"Siblings are the heartbeats of our childhood, always there in laughter, mischief, and love"

Can you share a funny or memorable childhood story about you and your siblings?

_____

_____

_____

_____

_____

_____

_____

_____

_____

_____

_____

_____

_____

_____

_____

_____

_____

NOTES

MEETING GRANDPA

MEETING GRANDPA

"The beginning of a love story is often written in the smallest, most memorable moments."

How did you and grandpa first meet? Was it love at first sight? Please share the story of how you met.

_____

_____

_____

_____

_____

_____

_____

_____

_____

_____

_____

_____

_____

_____

_____

_____

_____

MEETING GRANDPA

"In a single glance, we sometimes find a lifetime of companionship and adventure."

What was your first date like with Grandpa? Do you
remember what you did or talked about?

_____

_____

_____

_____

_____

_____

Did your parents approve of Grandpa when you first
introduced him? If so, why? If not, why?

_____

_____

_____

_____

_____

_____

_____

MEETING GRANDPA

"When you know, you know. Some moments just carry the certainty of forever."

How long did you date before getting married?

_____

When/how did you know that Grandpa was the one you
wanted to spend your life with?

_____

_____

_____

_____

_____

_____

How did Grandpa propose to you?

_____

_____

_____

_____

_____

_____

MEETING GRANDPA

"Together, we built memories that would last a lifetime and fill our hearts with joy."

What were some of your favorite memories together before getting married?

_____

_____

_____

_____

_____

_____

_____

What was the wedding ceremony like?
Any good wedding day stories?

_____

_____

_____

_____

_____

_____

_____

_____

MEETING GRANDPA

"Love is finding someone who feels like home, even in the smallest things."

In what ways do you think you and Grandpa are most alike?

_____

_____

_____

_____

_____

_____

_____

In what ways do you think you and Grandpa are total opposite?

_____

_____

_____

_____

_____

_____

_____

MEETING GRANDPA

"A true partner is someone who fills your life with unforgettable moments and treasured gifts."

How did you and Grandpa celebrate anniversaries or special milestones in your relationship?

_____

_____

_____

_____

_____

_____

What is one of the most romantic things
Grandpa has ever done for you?

_____

_____

_____

_____

_____

_____

_____

MEETING GRANDPA

"Loving you has been the easiest and most beautiful decision I've ever made."

What were some of the challenges you faced as a couple?

_____

_____

_____

_____

_____

_____

_____

What advice would you give to someone searching for
their perfect partner?

_____

_____

_____

_____

_____

_____

Do you have a "couple's bucket list"?
What are some of the things you have done together?

THINGS YOU'VE DONE TOGETHER

- [ ] ....
- [ ] ....
- [ ] ....
- [ ] ....
- [ ] ....
- [ ] ....
- [ ] ....
- [ ] ....
- [ ] ....
- [ ] ....
- [ ] ....
- [ ] ....

What's on your bucket list of things you still
dream of doing together or on your own?

B U C K E T   L I S T

- [ ] ....
- [ ] ....
- [ ] ....
- [ ] ....
- [ ] ....
- [ ] ....
- [ ] ....
- [ ] ....
- [ ] ....
- [ ] ....
- [ ] ....
- [ ] ....

BECOMING
A MOTHER

BECOMING A MOTHER

"Motherhood: All love begins and ends there."

How old were you when you first became a mother?

_____

How did you feel when you first found out
you were pregnant?

_____

_____

_____

_____

When you shared the news of your pregnancy, how did Grandpa
react? Do you remember anything special about that moment?

_____

_____

_____

_____

_____

_____

BECOMING A MOTHER

"Being a mother means that your heart is no longer yours; it wanders wherever your children go."

What do you remember most about your pregnancy? Did you face any challenges?

_____

_____

_____

_____

_____

_____

Did you have any food cravings? If yes, what were they?

_____

_____

_____

_____

_____

_____

BECOMING A MOTHER

"There is no way to be a perfect mother, but a million ways to be a good one."

Do you remember some of the advice you were
given as a new Mom?

_____

_____

_____

_____

_____

What were some of the biggest challenges
you faced as a new mother?

_____

_____

_____

_____

_____

_____

_____

BECOMING A MOTHER

"You are my heart, my soul, my everything. Being your mom is the greatest blessing of my life."

What parts of motherhood have brought you the most joy?

_____

_____

_____

_____

_____

_____

Looking back, is there anything you wish you had done differently as a mother?

_____

_____

_____

_____

_____

_____

NOTES

ABOUT YOUR KIDS

ABOUT YOUR KIDS

"Every child begins the world anew, bringing their own light and laughter."

What stands out the most in your memory about the day your children were born?

_____

_____

_____

_____

_____

_____

_____

How did you decide on each of your children's names?

_____

_____

_____

_____

_____

_____

_____

ABOUT YOUR KIDS

"The influence of a mother in the lives of her children is beyond calculation."
— James E. Faust

Did you have any other names in mind for your children, especially if they had been born the opposite gender?

_____

_____

_____

_____

_____

_____

_____

Do you remember which dishes you made that your kids enjoyed the most?

_____

_____

_____

_____

_____

ABOUT YOUR KIDS

"Sometimes the smallest things take up the most room in your heart."
– A.A. Milne

What is one of your most cherished memories of spending time
with your child/children when they were little?

_____

_____

_____

_____

_____

_____

_____

_____

_____

_____

_____

_____

_____

_____

_____

_____

_____

ABOUT YOUR KIDS

"Little moments, big memories."

Do you remember the bedtime stories your kids loved most?

_____

_____

_____

_____

_____

How would you describe each of your kids when they were little?

_____

_____

_____

_____

_____

_____

ABOUT YOUR KIDS

"Children are the living messages we send to a time we will not see."
— John F. Kennedy

What worked best to soothe your kids when they were upset?

_____

_____

_____

_____

_____

What's a funny memory of something one of your kids said or did when they were little?

_____

_____

_____

_____

_____

_____

_____

ABOUT YOUR KIDS

"Raising kids is a journey filled with moments to cherish, stories to tell, and memories that last a lifetime."

Do you remember anything your kids did that made you the angriest (even if it's funny now)?

_____

_____

_____

_____

_____

What is one family outing or vacation that you'll always remember?

_____

_____

_____

_____

_____

_____

_____

_____

_____

ABOUT YOUR KIDS

"The days are long, but the years are short." — Gretchen Rubin

How did you celebrate your kids' birthdays when they were little? Do you remember any especially memorable parties?

_____

_____

_____

_____

_____

Was there a moment when you felt like your children were growing up too fast?

_____

_____

_____

_____

_____

_____

ABOUT YOUR KIDS

"You will never outgrow my arms, no matter how big you get."

As your kids grew older, were there any challenging moments you faced as a parent? How did you handle them?

_____

_____

_____

_____

_____

_____

_____

What advice would you give to someone who is about to become a new mother?

_____

_____

_____

_____

_____

"The moment a child
is born, the mother
is also born."

— Osho

NOTES

YOU TAUGHT ME I CAN FLY.

Love you Grandma!

10

BECOMING
A GRANDMA

BECOMING A GRANDMOTHER

"Becoming a grandmother is the greatest joy, a second chance to love unconditionally."

How old were you when you first became a grandmother?

_____

How many grandchildren do you have?

_____

What are the names and ages of all your grandchildren?

_____

_____

_____

_____

_____

_____

_____

_____

_____

_____

BECOMING A GRANDMTHER

A grandmother's nickname is often a badge of love, spoken from
the heart of a grandchild."

What do your grandchildren call you?
Is there a special name they use?

_____

_____

_____

What was it like when you found out you were going to
be a grandmother for the first time?

_____

_____

_____

_____

_____

What do you enjoy most about being a grandmother?

_____

_____

_____

_____

_____

_____

BECOMING A GRANDMOTHER

"Grandmothers are a bridge of wisdom, guiding both parents and grandchildren with love."

"What is one piece of advice you've shared with your children about parenting?"

_____

_____

_____

_____

_____

_____

_____

What family traditions do you want your grandchildren to carry on?

_____

_____

_____

_____

_____

_____

BECOMING A GRANDMOTHER

"Grandchildren fill a space in your heart you never knew was
empty, often with laughter and surprises.

What's the most memorable or funny moment you've had with your grandchildren?

_____

_____

_____

_____

_____

_____

_____

_____

_____

_____

_____

_____

_____

_____

"Being a grandmother is the greatest joy in life. One moment you're just a mother. The next, you're all-wise and prehistoric."
– Pam Brown

WORKING THROUGH THE YEARS

WORKING THROUGH THE YEARS

"When I was a child, I had dreams of who I would become. But being your mother has been the greatest dream come true."

When you were a kid, what did you want to be when you grew up?

_____

_____

_____

What was your first job, and how old were you?

_____

how much were you paid?
What did you do with your first paycheck?

_____

_____

_____

_____

How many jobs did you have before you got married?

_____

_____

_____

WORKING THROUGH THE YEARS

"No job can ever compare to the love and work it takes to raise you. It's the hardest and most rewarding work of my life."

What was the best job you ever had, and what made it so special?

_____

_____

_____

_____

_____

How did you balance work and family when your children were little, especially during hard times?

_____

_____

_____

_____

_____

_____

_____

_____

WORKING THROUGH THE YEARS

"My greatest accomplishments aren't on my resume; they're in the hearts of the children I raised."

Have you had a boss or mentor who made a positive impact on you? What made them stand out?

_____

_____

_____

_____

What's one career decision you'd change if you could, and why?

_____

_____

_____

_____

What do you consider to be important work ethics?

_____

_____

_____

_____

WORKING THROUGH THE YEARS

"The most important work ethic I've learned is love, because in both work and family, love keeps you going when times get tough."

What advice would you give to someone just starting their career?

_____

_____

_____

_____

_____

_____

If you could write a letter to your younger self about your career journey, what would you say?

_____

_____

_____

_____

_____

_____

_____

"A grandmother is a safe haven in a world of storms."

LIFE LESSONS
AND
BELIEFS

LIFE LESSONS AND BELIEFS

"Believe in the power of hope, faith, and the lessons life has to offer."

Do you believe in miracles? Has there been anything in your life that you consider a miracle?

_____

_____

_____

_____

_____

How has religion or spirituality influenced your life and values?

_____

_____

_____

_____

_____

_____

_____

LIFE LESSONS AND BELIEFS

"It's not what we have in life, but who we have in our life that matters." – Unknown

Have you ever experienced a moment that completely
changed your perspective on life? What happened?

_____

_____

_____

_____

_____

_____

Do you believe in life after death?
If so, who is the person you'd most like to meet?

_____

_____

_____

_____

_____

_____

LIFE LESSONS AND BELIEFS

"Success is not what we achieve, but the love and memories we leave behind in the hearts of our children."

Have you ever forgiven someone who was really hard to forgive? If so, can you share your story?

_____

_____

_____

_____

_____

_____

If you could pass on a single piece of wisdom to your grandchildren, what would it be and why?

_____

_____

_____

_____

_____

_____

_____

LIFE LESSONS AND BELIEFS

"Faith is the bird that feels the light and sings when the dawn is still dark."

How do you stay positive and motivated when things get tough?

_____

_____

_____

_____

_____

If you could create a new family tradition, what
would it be and why?

_____

_____

_____

_____

_____

_____

LIFE LESSONS AND BELIEFS

In the end, it's not the years in your life that count. It's the life
in your years." – Abraham Lincoln

What does happiness mean to you, and how has your definition of happiness changed throughout your life?

_____

_____

_____

_____

_____

_____

_____

_____

_____

_____

_____

_____

_____

_____

13

HOPES
AND
WISDOM

HOPES AND WISDOM

"Wisdom is a treasure passed through generations, enriching each life it touches."

What do you think is the most important quality a person can have?

_____

_____

_____

_____

_____

What is the one mistake you made that you never want
your children to make?

_____

_____

_____

_____

_____

_____

_____

_____

HOPES AND WISDOM

"My hope for you is that you see the beauty in life, cherish the moments, and always keep dreaming." – Unknown

Do you have any regrets about things not done or learned?

_____

_____

_____

_____

_____

Is there anything you now realize was not worth worrying about?

_____

_____

_____

_____

_____

_____

_____

_____

HOPES AND WISDOM

"In the garden of life, we plant seeds of hope and nurture them with lessons learned."

Looking back, what is one decision you are most proud of, and why?

_____

_____

_____

_____

_____

If you could relive any moment from your life,
what would it be and why?

_____

_____

_____

_____

_____

_____

_____

_____

_____

HOPES AND WISDOM

"The strength to dream and the courage to pursue it are the greatest gifts we can leave behind."

What are the three things you are most grateful for in your life?

_____

_____

_____

How do you want to be remembered by your
family and friends?

_____

_____

_____

_____

_____

_____

_____

_____

HOPES AND WISDOM

"To my children, I give my love, my hopes, and my wisdom, knowing that they will carry it with them always."

If you could host a dinner party with any three people, living or deceased, who would you invite?

_____

_____

_____

What are your wishes for your children's futures?

_____

_____

_____

_____

_____

_____

_____

_____

_____

_____

HOPES AND WISDOM

"A parent's wisdom is the quiet voice that guides you through life, long after you've stopped asking for it." – Unknown

If you could leave a time capsule for future generations, what three items would you put in it and why?

_____

_____

_____

_____

_____

_____

_____

_____

_____

_____

_____

_____

HOPES AND WISDOM

"The strength to dream and the courage to pursue it are the greatest gifts we can leave behind."

If you could give one piece of advice to your younger self, what would it be and why?

_____

_____

_____

_____

_____

_____

_____

_____

_____

_____

_____

_____

_____

GRANDMA'S TRIVIA

If you could live anywhere in the world,
where would it be and why?

_____

_____

_____

_____

If you could magically learn a new language overnight, which one
would you choose and why?

_____

_____

_____

_____

What is your all-time favorite movie or TV show, and why
do you love it so much?

_____

_____

_____

_____

GRANDMA'S TRIVIA

If you could travel back in time, which era
would you visit and why?

_____

_____

_____

_____

_____

If you could switch lives with any fictional character, who
would it be and why?

_____

_____

_____

_____

If you were leader of a country, what would be the first
law you would introduce?

_____

_____

_____

"Every laugh, every story, and every moment we've shared is a treasure. Thank you, Grandma, for the love, wisdom, and kindness you've given me. I'm forever grateful for the beautiful life lessons you've passed down to me."

JUST FOR FUN

JUST FOR FUN

If you won a $10 million lottery, what would you
want to do with the money?

_____

_____

_____

_____

If you could have dinner with any celebrity—past or
present—who would it be, and why?

_____

_____

_____

_____

_____

_____

_____

_____

JUST FOR FUN ☺

If you could be any animal for a day, what would you be and why?

_____

_____

_____

_____

_____

If you could live on a deserted island and bring only 5
things, what would they be?

_____

_____

_____

_____

What is the most memorable gift you have ever received?

_____

_____

_____

JUST FOR FUN

What is the most embarrassing Moment of your life?

_____

_____

_____

_____

_____

_____

What is the funniest thing that's ever happened to you or
that you've ever witnessed?

_____

_____

_____

_____

_____

JUST FOR FUN

If you could do any job in the world, without worrying about qualifications or salary, what would it be and why?

_____

_____

_____

_____

_____

_____

_____

If you could have any celebrity play you in a movie, who would it be and why?

_____

_____

_____

_____

_____

_____

JUST FOR FUN

What is your favorite thing to do on a lazy day?

_____

_____

_____

_____

_____

_____

_____

If you could only watch one TV show or movie for the rest
of your life, what would it be and why?

_____

_____

_____

_____

_____

_____

"To the world, you
are a grandma.
To our family, you
are the world."
— Unknown

LITTLE DETAILS ABOUT YOU

1   What time do you usually wake up?

2   What time do you usually go to bed?

3   How do you like your eggs?

4   What's your favorite ice cream flavor?

5   How do you like your coffee?

A LITTLE MORE
ABOUT YOU

What is your natural hair color?
What has it been over the years?

_____

_____

_____

If you wear glasses, how old were you when you
got your first pair?

_____

Do you have any allergies? If so, what are they?

_____

_____

_____

Did you ever have a funny or memorable
experience at the dentist?

_____

_____

_____

_____

_____

A LITTLE MORE
ABOUT YOU

When was your first time in hospital?
Do you remember why you went?

_____

_____

_____

_____

_____

Have you ever been in an accident or had a close call?
If so, what happened?

_____

_____

_____

_____

_____

_____

_____

_____

Message
(Today) PM 12:21

"What do you want me to remember as I grow up?"

"As you grow up, remember to be kind, to yourself and others. Don't be afraid of mistakes—they help you grow. When life gets tough, know you're stronger than you think, and I'll always be proud of you. Dream big, work hard, and never forget that you are deeply loved. You've got this."

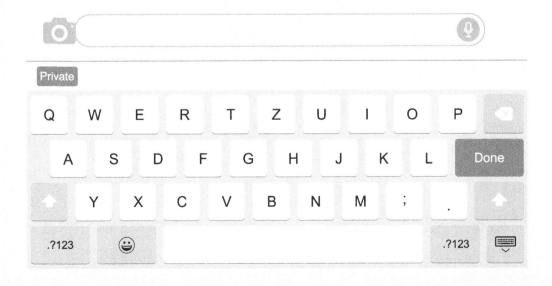

Add your favorite
photo here

More Stories to Share

_____

_____

_____

_____

_____

_____

_____

_____

_____

_____

_____

_____

_____

_____

More Stories to Share

Woocee Designs

Made in the USA
Las Vegas, NV
17 April 2025

21054877R00079